AUTO TECHNICIAN

COOL VOCATIONAL CAREERS

Published in the United States of America by Cherry Lake Publishing
Ann Arbor, Michigan
www.cherrylakepublishing.com

Content Adviser: Allen Day, Automotive Services Instructor, Washtenaw Community College, Ann Arbor, Michigan
Reading Adviser: Marla Conn MS, Ed., Literacy specialist, Read-Ability, Inc.

Photo Credits: © Sudhee Sakthan/Shutterstock, cover, 1, 16; © Jupiterimages/Thinkstock, 5; © VMarin/Shutterstock, 6;
© kurhan/Shutterstock, 8; © wavebreakmedia/Shutterstock, 9; © XiXinXing/Shutterstock, 10; © Pavel L/ Photo and Video/
Shutterstock, 13; © 4x6/istock, 14; © gilaxia/istock, 17; © Monkey Business Images/Shutterstock, 18, 26;
© goodluz/Shutterstock, 21; © sturti/istock, 22; © kaczor58/Shutterstock, 25; © Rido/Shuttestock, 28; © Mcity, 29

Library of Congress Cataloging-in-Publication Data
CIP data has been filed and is available at catalog.loc.gov.

Cherry Lake Publishing would like to acknowledge the work of the Partnership for 21st Century Learning.
Please visit *www.p21.org* for more information.

Printed in the United States of America
Corporate Graphics

ABOUT THE AUTHOR

Ellen Labrecque is a freelance writer living in Yardley, Pennsylvania. Previously, she was a senior editor at *Sports Illustrated Kids*. Ellen loves to travel and then learn about new places and people she can write about in her books.

TABLE OF CONTENTS

CHAPTER 1

On the Road Again

Anya and Jack sat in the backseat of their minivan, ready to begin their trip. Their family was driving to the beach for the day! Their father pushed the starter button, but nothing happened. He tried again. Still nothing.

"Time to call a tow truck," he said. They needed to visit Mr. Ritchie for help repairing the van. Mr. Ritchie was the local auto technician.

Anya, Jack, and their father rode along with the driver in the tow truck. They took the van into the garage. Mr. Ritchie examined the van carefully. Anya and Jack hoped they would still be able to drive to the beach. Finally, Mr. Ritchie stepped outside to talk to them.

Sometimes car trouble can ruin your plans for the day.

Cars that start without keys are becoming more common.

"I figured out what the problem is," he said. "The **battery** is dead. It needs to be replaced. The job will cost about $200. Do you want me to go ahead and install it?" Anya and Jack's father said yes and thanked Mr. Ritchie for his help. Soon, the car was fixed. Mr. Ritchie explained the charges on the bill for the new part and the work, called labor. It was time to hit the road. They could still go to the beach after all!

Anya and Jack learned that auto technicians have very important jobs. They are responsible for maintaining and repairing the vehicles that people rely on. Sometimes these workers are called auto mechanics.

Auto technicians need the skills to solve a variety of technical mysteries—and quickly! Like Anya and Jack's father, some people have trouble getting their cars to start. Some people hear strange sounds coming from the engine. Others have problems with their brakes.

21st Century Content

Most new cars today no longer start with keys. They start with the push of a button.

Even though car keys were invented in the 1920s and have been commonly used since the 1950s, "eventually the key will go away," predicts Dave Sullivan, who works at a car researching company.

Car companies say push-button starters are safer than keys. That's because keys can be bumped and cars can accidentally get turned off while on the road. But technicians still have to know how the push buttons work in case they break. It is a whole new skill set they need to learn.

Technicians often use computers to diagnose a car's problems.

Auto technicians **diagnose** the cause of these problems. They use everything from wrenches to computers to figure out what is wrong. Auto technicians also depend on **feedback** from customers. It is important for technicians to ask the right questions. This helps them gather clues so they can decide what needs to be fixed. Then they make the necessary repairs.

Auto technicians need to be able to communicate clearly and openly with their customers. They have to provide **estimates** of how much a job will cost and how long it will take. Owners want

Before starting a job, a technician gives the car owner an estimate of the cost.

Cars need oil changes a few times a year.

their vehicles back as soon as possible. They need to drive to work, school, and, of course, the beach!

Auto technicians encourage drivers to bring in their vehicles for routine maintenance. This is like taking your car for a checkup every couple of months. During routine maintenance, auto technicians often rotate tires so they wear evenly. They also put fresh oil in the car, which is called an **oil change**. Oil keeps the engine from wearing out.

Many auto technicians work on a variety of vehicles. Others work only with a particular make of car, such as a Ford or Toyota. Some technicians deal only with certain parts of a car. For example, some focus on the body. Others handle problems inside each car's interior. Other technicians fix engines and **transmissions**. No matter what kind of work they do, auto technicians usually have a busy schedule at the garage!

CHAPTER 2

Car Doctors

Like a doctor, the auto technician must identify why the car is sick. He or she relies on several different tools to help diagnose the exact cause of the trouble. He or she often raises the car on a **lift** in order to examine the car from underneath. He or she uses basic hand tools such as screwdrivers, pliers, and wrenches. But more and more, auto technicians also use special computers as well as wireless devices that link up to the car's onboard diagnostic (OBD) system. OBD is a diagnostic system built into the car that helps mechanics determine what isn't working in the car.

Sean has a portable computer plugged into the OBD of a car that a customer brought into his garage. The customer told Sean his car has been shutting down for no reason. Thanks to the help of the computer, Sean soon figures out why. One of the parts in

A lift helps a technician work underneath a car.

the car has a hairline crack in an ignition **coil**. Unwanted water and **condensation** have been seeping through. Without the computer, it could have taken Sean as long as 8 hours to figure out what the problem was with the car. Using the scan tool, it took him just 30 minutes.

Innovation has changed the job of auto technicians. All of the cars today are computerized. They have some of the latest technologies, which include things such as navigation equipment. This means auto technicians are using computers as much as they are using tools like wrenches and screwdrivers.

Auto technicians need to communicate well with their customers.

Once Sean figured out what the problem was, he called his customer and told him the coil in his car had to be replaced. Sean said the cost of the coil, plus the labor, would be $300.

Sean fixes about nine cars a day. Auto technicians get very busy when a lot of customers all need work done at the same time. Their schedules depend on how big their garages are and how many other people work there. Different kinds of jobs can also affect a technician's schedule. Some repairs take much longer than others. This means a technician's schedule can change from day to day. He or she gets paid per hour, and those numbers change depending on how many cars come into the shop. Many garages are open evenings and weekends to fit their customers' schedules.

Auto technicians do other things besides fix cars. They talk with parts suppliers. Mechanics don't always have new car parts in their garage. They have to call a parts supplier and order it.

They also talk with customers. It is important for them to be polite but get information quickly. They must ask detailed questions and pay careful attention to the answers. First, they try to figure out how long the customer has been having car

Life and Career Skills

Once auto technicians graduate from technical school, they are encouraged to keep learning new skills as mechanics. They are encouraged to take online classes, attend live seminars, and study the newest technology. Why is it important for mechanics to keep learning things in their field? Do you think this is important to do in any type of career? Why or why not?

Owners should take their cars in for routine maintenance checkups.

A technician might be able to fix the problem without ordering more supplies.

problems. Then they ask if the customer has noticed anything unusual about the way the vehicle has been running. Is it making odd noises? They also ask for the date of the car's last routine maintenance checkup.

Sometimes customers have simple requests. They may just want an oil change. The request can sometimes be more complex, though. A customer might know that her car is not working properly but not be able to explain the problem.

Once the technician diagnoses the problem, he figures out how to correct it. Sometimes he can make the repair in-house, if

Technicians wear safety glasses to protect their eyes.

that garage keeps a supply of parts for common repairs. Other times, the technician may have to order parts from the dealerships that stock and sell them. Either way, he contacts the customer first to tell them how much the repair will cost. If the customer agrees to the estimate, the auto technician begins work.

The work might involve anything from fixing a **radiator** leak to replacing the brakes. Such jobs are often messy. It is common for auto technicians to handle greasy or dirty parts, so they wear washable uniforms and disposable gloves. Most put on safety glasses to keep metal shavings or automotive fluids from getting in their eyes. It is important to be safe in the garage.

After the technician completes a job, the garage's service writer calls the customer to tell them their car is ready. This person often acts as the connection between the technician and the customer. He or she explains everything the technician did, what problems came up, and how they were fixed. The customer gets a work order from the technician, which outlines all of the parts and labor involved.

The workday ends when the mechanic finally watches the last customer of the day drive away from the garage. Then it is time to put away the tools and prepare for the next morning.

CHAPTER 3

Becoming an Auto Technician

There were about 250 million cars on the road in the United States in 2015. That is *a lot* of cars to keep safely running. With this large number of vehicles, it's not surprising that auto technicians are more in demand than ever before!

The best way to become an auto technician is to graduate high school and then attend a **technical school**. Training for a career as a technician is more challenging than it has ever been. Car technology is changing at an amazing rate. New vehicles have many computer-controlled systems. Technical schools are constantly updating their programs to keep up with the latest technology. Part of an auto technician's education takes place in a classroom. Some of it also occurs in an auto shop. This allows students to apply their skills to real-life situations.

Students in technical school can learn the basics of car repair.

Technical school usually lasts for one to two years, but learning new skills as an auto technician happens throughout an entire career. Auto technicians will watch videos, take online classes, and attend live training classes and clinics to make sure their skills remain sharp.

How can you decide which technical school is right for you? The National Automotive Technicians Education Foundation (NATEF) can help make your choice easier. NATEF accredits auto technician training programs. In other words, it makes sure schools meet the standards set by the auto industry.

How much a technician earns depends on his or her skills and experience.

More than 2,250 programs in the United States are accredited by NATEF.

Auto technicians can also take special classes and tests to receive National Institute for Automotive Service Excellence (ASE) certification. This helps them stand out in the field. ASE-certified technicians are sometimes able to advance in their careers more quickly than others.

Even these professionals do not usually start off running their own garages and shops. Many work as assistants to more established auto technicians for a few years. Then they find higher-paying jobs as technicians, practicing simple repairs and maintenance. They gain experience by taking on more and more difficult tasks.

Auto technicians can make anywhere from $16 to $25 per hour. Their earnings partially depend on which skills they have and how much professional training they have had.

Life and Career Skills

Auto technicians need to have strong science and math skills to do their job and do it well. Here's a math problem for you. If an auto technician makes $20 an hour and works 40 hours a week, how much does he make each week? How much does he make in a year? (Here's a clue: There are 52 weeks in a year).

CHAPTER 4

High Tech

Vehicles are changing rapidly as technology continues to advance. Almost every system, including the brakes, steering wheel, and seats, is operated, at least partly, by a computer. Everything is connected by wires. Fixing cars has gone high tech. For an auto mechanic, a computer is as important a tool as a wrench.

"Today more than ever, auto service and repair technicians need to understand computers, math, science, and how to talk to people," says Trish Serratore, president of NATEF. "Cars have more electronics than ever and need smart people to fix them."

The U.S. Department of Labor estimates that employment opportunities for auto technicians are increasing. Around 124,800 jobs will be added by 2020, for a total of 848,200

New technology is always being developed.

Car owners want their vehicles to run safely and easily.

positions. The most sought-after technicians will be the "master mechanics" who can use computers to find and then fix the car's problems. Why are these new technicians needed?

First, the number of vehicles being driven in the United States continues to rise. This means more auto technicians are needed to perform maintenance tasks and repairs. In addition, automakers are building vehicles to last longer. The average cost of a new car is more than $30,000. People spending this much money want a car they can trust! In 2015, the average car on the road was 11 years old. Drivers rely on professionals to help them care for these long-lasting cars.

Auto technicians still have to prove themselves in order to get the best jobs. Many employers want to hire workers with specialized training. They also want people who are familiar with computers and can handle other fast-paced changes that are shaping the auto industry. Auto technicians who are not ASE certified or who do not have a formal education may find it harder to compete.

The future is sure to be exciting for auto technicians. People rely on their cars to get around and enjoy their lives. There will always be a demand for professionals who care for vehicles. Do you see yourself wearing an auto technician's uniform one day?

As long as there are cars, there will be a need for auto technicians.

Mcity is a fake city for testing connected and automated cars.

21st Century Content

What's the population of Mcity, Michigan? Zero, but Mcity is still all about cars! Mcity is a test facility in Ann Arbor where researchers can test "connected and automated" vehicles. Connected cars use wireless communication to gather data about the location, speed, and direction of surrounding traffic. Automated cars can do some things, such as parking, without a driver. A fully automated car doesn't need a driver at all! Mcity has two-, three-, and four-lane roads, and roads made of different materials like concrete and gravel, so new technology can be tested like it's real life. There are even sidewalks and streetlamps. This way, researchers can improve how the cars function in a safe space before they're tried out in public. Check out www.mtc.umich.edu to learn more!

Think About It

Ask your mom or dad if they have an auto technician that they trust to fix their car. What do they like about their auto technician? Why do they trust him or her?

Do you think the job of auto technician will continue to change in the future? What other skills could auto technicians eventually need to know?

What kind of car would you like to own someday? Go online to learn more about it. How much does it cost? What colors does it come in? How has the design changed over the years?

For More Information

BOOKS

DK Publishing. *Car: The Definitive Visual History of the Automobile.* New York: DK Publishing, 2011.

Eason, Sarah. *How Does a Car Work?* New York: Gareth Stevens Publishing, 2010.

Kenney, Karen Latchana. *What Makes Vehicles Safer?* Minneapolis: Lerner Publications, 2016.

WEB SITES

How Stuff Works: Auto
http://auto.howstuffworks.com/engine.htm
Read this article to learn how car engines work.

Learn How to Become: Mechanic
http://www.learnhowtobecome.org/mechanic/
Check out this Web page to learn more about becoming an auto technician.

GLOSSARY

battery (BAT-uh-ree) part of a car that powers the starter motor and all the other electronics in the car; it also stores energy to start the car

coil (KOIL) the part of a car's engine that transforms the battery's energy into sparks that can ignite the fuel to start the car

condensation (kahn-den-SAY-shuhn) the changing of a gas or vapor into its liquid form

diagnose (dye-uhg-NOHS) to determine the cause of a problem

estimates (ES-tuh-muhts) approximate calculations of how much something will cost

feedback (FEED-bak) information or criticism that is given to help improve something

innovation (in-uh-VAY-shuhn) something new or different that is introduced

lift (LIFT) a machine used to raise a car into the air so its bottom and interior can be viewed more clearly; also called a hoist

oil change (OIL CHAYNJ) putting fresh oil into a car's engine

radiator (RAY-dee-ay-tuhr) a series of tubes through which hot liquid circulates, sending heat out

technical school (TEK-nih-kuhl SKOOL) a school that offers courses and training to prepare students for mechanical and industrial careers

transmissions (trans-MIH-shuhnz) systems of parts, including gears, that send power from a car's engine to its axle

INDEX